The Beginning and The End

AND OTHER POEMS

Robinson Jeffers

The Beginning
& THE END
AND OTHER POEMS

 Random House

New York

FOURTH PRINTING

MANUFACTURED IN THE UNITED STATES OF AMERICA

Design by Tere LoPrete

The publisher wishes to thank Steuben Glass for providing the text of "Birds and Fishes," from their Poetry in Crystal exhibit.

Contents

The Root of

All Things

———

The Great Explosion

The universe expands and contracts like a great heart.
It is expanding, the farthest nebulae
Rush with the speed of light into empty space.
It will contract, the immense navies of stars and galaxies,
    dust-clouds and nebulae
Are recalled home, they crush against each other in one
    harbor, they stick in one lump
And then explode it, nothing can hold them down; there
    is no way to express that explosion; all that exists
Roars into flame, the tortured fragments rush away from
    each other into all the sky, new universes
Jewel the black breast of night; and far off the outer neb-
    ulae like charging spearmen again
Invade emptiness.
               No wonder we are so fascinated with
    fire-works
And our huge bombs: it is a kind of homesickness per-
    haps for the howling fire-blast that we were born
    from.

But the whole sum of the energies
That made and contained the giant atom survives. It will
    gather again and pile up, the power and the glory—
And no doubt it will burst again: diastole and systole:
    the whole universe beats like a heart.
Peace in our time was never one of God's promises; but
    back and forth, die and live, burn and be damned,
The great heart beating, pumping into our arteries His
    terrible life.

He is beautiful beyond belief.
And we, God's apes—or tragic children—share in the
    beauty. We see it above our torment, that's what
    life's for.
He is no God of love, no justice of a little city like
    Dante's Florence, no anthropoid God
Making commandments: this is the God who does not
    care and will never cease. Look at the seas there
Flashing against this rock in the darkness—look at the
    tide-stream stars—and the fall of nations—and
    dawn
Wandering with wet white feet down the Carmel Valley
    to meet the sea. These are real and we see their
    beauty.
The great explosion is probably only a metaphor—I know
    not—of faceless violence, the root of all things.

The Beginning and the End

The unformed volcanic earth, a female thing,
Furiously following with the other planets
Their lord the sun: her body is molten metal pressed
    rigid
By its own mass; her beautiful skin, basalt and granite
    and the lighter elements,
Swam to the top. She was like a mare in her heat eyeing
    the stallion,
Screaming for life in the womb; her atmosphere
Was the breath of her passion: not the blithe air
Men breathe and live, but marsh-gas, ammonia, sul-
    phured hydrogen,
Such poison as our remembering bodies return to
When they die and decay and the end of life
Meets its beginning. The sun heard her and stirred
Her thick air with fierce lightnings and flagellations
Of germinal power, building impossible molecules,
    amino-acids
And flashy unstable proteins: thence life was born,
Its nitrogen from ammonia, carbon from methane,
Water from the cloud and salts from the young seas,
It dribbled down into the primal ocean like a babe's
    urine
Soaking the cloth: heavily built protein molecules
Chemically growing, bursting apart as the tensions
In the inordinate molecule become unbearable—
That is to say, growing and reproducing themselves, a
    virus
On the warm ocean.

Time and the world changed,
The proteins were no longer created, the ammoniac at-
    mosphere
And the great storms no more. This virus now
Must labor to maintain itself. It clung together
Into bundles of life, which we call cells,
With microscopic walls enclosing themselves
Against the world. But why would life maintain itself,
Being nothing but a dirty scum on the sea
Dropped from foul air? Could it perhaps perceive
Glories to come? Could it foresee that cellular life
Would make the mountain forest and the eagle dawning,
Monstrously beautiful, wings, eyes and claws, dawning
Over the rock-ridge? And the passionate human intelli-
    gence
Straining its limits, striving to understand itself and the
    universe to the last galaxy—
Flammantia moenia mundi, Lucretius wrote,
Alliterating like a Saxon—all those Ms mean majesty—
The flaming world-walls, far-flung fortifications of being
Against not-being.
                    For after a time the cells of life
Bound themselves into clans, a multitude of cells
To make one being—as the molecules before
Had made of many one cell. Meanwhile they had in-
    vented
Chlorophyll and ate sunlight, cradled in peace
On the warm waves; but certain assassins among them
Discovered that it was easier to eat flesh
Than feed on lean air and sunlight: thence the animals,

Greedy mouths and guts, life robbing life,
Grew from the plants; and as the ocean ebbed and
flowed many plants and animals
Were stranded in the great marshes along the shore,
Where many died and some lived. From these grew all
land-life,
Plants, beasts and men; the mountain forest and the
mind of Aeschylus
And the mouse in the wall.

What is this thing called life? —But I believe
That the earth and stars too, and the whole glittering
universe, and rocks on the mountain have life,
Only we do not call it so—I speak of the life
That oxydizes fats and proteins and carbo-
Hydrates to live on, and from that chemical energy
Makes pleasure and pain, wonder, love, adoration, hatred
and terror: how do these thing grow
From a chemical reaction?
                                          I think they were here al-
ready. I think the rocks
And the earth and the other planets, and the stars and
galaxies
Have their various consciousness, all things are conscious;
But the nerves of an animal, the nerves and brain
Bring it to focus; the nerves and brain are like a burning-
glass
To concentrate the heat and make it catch fire:
It seems to us martyrs hotter than the blazing hearth

From which it came. So we scream and laugh, clamorous
    animals
Born howling to die groaning: the old stones in the door-
    yard
Prefer silence: but those and all things have their own
    awareness,
As the cells of a man have; they feel and feed and in-
    fluence each other, each unto all,
Like the cells of a man's body making one being,
They make one being, one consciousness, one life, one
    God.

But whence came the race of man? I will make a guess.
A change of climate killed the great northern forests,
Forcing the manlike apes down from their trees,
They starved up there. They had been secure up there,
But famine is no security: among the withered branches
    blue famine:
They had to go down to the earth, where green still grew
And small meats might be gleaned. But there the great
    flesh-eaters,
Tiger and panther and the horrible fumbling bear and
    endless wolf-packs made life
A dream of death. Therefore man has these dreams,
And kills out of pure terror. Therefore man walks erect,
Forever alerted: as the bear rises to fight
So man does always. Therefore he invented fire and flint
    weapons
In his desperate need. Therefore he is cruel and bloody-
    handed and quick-witted, having survived
Against all odds. Never blame the man: his hard-pressed

Ancestors formed him: the other anthropoid apes were
    safe
In the great southern rain-forest and hardly changed
In a million years: but the race of man was made
By shock and agony. Therefore they invented the song
    called language
To celebrate their survival and record their deeds. And
    therefore the deeds they celebrate—
Achilles raging in the flame of the south, Baltic Beowulf
    like a fog-blinded sea-bear
Prowling the blasted fenland in the bleak twilight to the
    black water—
Are cruel and bloody. Epic, drama and history,
Jesus and Judas, Jenghiz, Julius Caesar, no great poem
Without the blood-splash. They are a little lower than
    the angels, as someone said. —Blood-snuffing rats:
But never blame them: a wound was made in the brain
When life became too hard, and has never healed.
It is there that they learned trembling religion and blood-
    sacrifice,
It is there that they learned to butcher beasts and to
    slaughter men,
And hate the world: the great religions of love and kind-
    ness
May conceal that, not change it. They are not primary
    but reactions
Against the hate: as the eye after feeding on a red sunfall
Will see green suns.
                        The human race is one of God's
    sense-organs,
Immoderately alerted to feel good and evil

And pain and pleasure. It is a nerve-ending,
Like eye, ear, taste-buds (hardly able to endure
The nauseous draught) it is a sensory organ of God's.
As Titan-mooded Lear or Prometheus reveal to their
    audience
Extremes of pain and passion they will never find
In their own lives but through the poems as sense-organs
They feel and know them: so the exultations and agonies
    of beasts and men
Are sense-organs of God: and on other globes
Throughout the universe much greater nerve-endings
Enrich the consciousness of the one being
Who is all that exists. This is man's mission:
To find and feel; all animal experience
Is a part of God's life. He would be balanced and neutral
As a rock on the shore, but the red sunset-waves
Of life's passions fling over him. He endures them,
We endure ours. That ancient wound in the brain
Has never healed, it hangs wide, it lets in the stars
Into the animal-stinking ghost-ridden darkness, the hu-
    man soul.
The mind of man. . . .
Slowly, perhaps, man may grow into it—
Do you think so? This villainous king of beasts, this de-
    formed ape? —He has mind
And imagination, he might go far
And end in honor. The hawks are more heroic but man
    has a steeper mind,
Huge pits of darkness, high peaks of light,
You may calculate a comet's orbit or the dive of a hawk,
    not a man's mind.

The Great Wound

At the near approach of a star—huge tides
Agitated the molten surface of the earth.
The tides grew higher as it passed. It tore from the earth
The top of one great wave: the moon was torn
Out of the Pacific basin: the cold white stone that lights
    us at night
Left that great wound in the earth, the Pacific Ocean
With all its islands and navies. I can stand on the cliff
    here
And hear the half-molten basalt and granite tearing apart
    and see that huge bird
Leaping up to her star. But the star passed,
The moon remained, circling her ancient home,
Dragging the sea-tides after her, haggard with loneliness.

The mathematicians and physics men
Have their mythology; they work alongside the truth,
Never touching it; their equations are false
But the things *work*. Or, when gross error appears,
They invent new ones; they drop the theory of waves
In universal ether and imagine curved space.
Nevertheless their equations bombed Hiroshima.
The terrible things *worked*.
                    The poet also
Has his mythology. He tells you the moon arose
Out of the Pacific basin. He tells you that Troy was
    burnt for a vagrant
Beautiful woman, whose face launched a thousand ships.
It is unlikely: it might be true: but church and state

Depend on more peculiarly impossible myths:
That all men are born free and equal: consider that!
And that a wandering Hebrew poet named Jesus
Is the God of the universe. Consider that!

Passenger Pigeons

Slowly the passenger pigeons increased, then suddenly
    their numbers
Became enormous, they would flatten ten miles of forest
When they flew down to roost, and the cloud of their
    rising
Eclipsed the dawns. They became too many, they are all
    dead,
Not one remains.
              And the American bison: their hordes
Would hide a prairie from horizon to horizon, great
    heads and storm-cloud shoulders, a torrent of life—
How many are left? For a time, for a few years, their
    bones
Turned the dark prairies white.
             You, Death, you watch
    for these things,
These explosions of life: they are your food,
They make your feasts.
             But turn your great rolling eyes
    away from humanity,
Those grossly craving black eyes. It is true we increase.
A man from Britain landing in Gaul when Rome had
    fallen,
He journeyed fourteen days inland through that beauti-
    ful
Rich land, the orchards and rivers and the looted villas:
    he reports that he saw
No living man. But now we fill up the gaps,

In spite of wars, famines and pestilences we are quite
suddenly
Three billion people: our bones, ours too, would make
Wide prairies white, a beautiful snow of unburied bones:
Bones that have twitched and quivered in the nights of
love,
Bones that have been shaken with laughter and hung
slack in sorrow, coward bones
Worn out with trembling, strong bones broken on the
rack, bones broken in battle,
Broad bones gnarled with hard labor, and the little bones
of sweet young children, and the white empty
skulls,
Little carved ivory wine-jugs that used to contain
Passion and thought and love and insane delirium, where
now
Not even worms live.
                Respect humanity, Death, these
shameless black eyes of yours,
It is not necessary to take all at once—besides that, you
cannot do it, we are too powerful,
We are men, not pigeons; you may take the old, the useless and helpless, the cancer-bitten and the tender
young,
But the human race has still history to make. For look—
look now
At our achievements: we have bridled the cloud-leaper
lightning, a lion whipped by a man, to carry our
messages
And work our will, we have snatched the live thunder-
bolt

Out of God's hands. Ha? That was little and last year—
    for now we have taken
The primal powers, creation and annihilation; we make
    new elements, such as God never saw,
We can explode atoms and annul the fragments, nothing
    left but pure energy, we shall use it
In peace and war—"Very clever," he answered, in his
    thin piping voice,
Cruel and a eunuch.
                    Roll those idiot black eyes of yours
On the field-beasts, not on intelligent man,
We are not in your order. You watched the dinosaurs
Grow into horror: they had been little efts in the ditches
    and presently became enormous, with leaping flanks
And tearing teeth, plated with armor, nothing could
    stand against them, nothing but you,
Death, and they died. You watched the sabre-tooth tigers
Develop those huge fangs, unnecessary as our sciences,
    and presently they died. You have their bones
In the oil-pits and layer-rock, you will not have ours.
    With pain and wonder and labor we have bought
    intelligence.
We have minds like the tusks of those forgotten tigers,
    hypertrophied and terrible,
We have counted the stars and half understood them, we
    have watched the farther galaxies fleeing away
    from us, wild herds
Of panic horses—or a trick of distance deceived the
    prism—we outfly falcons and eagles and meteors,
Faster than sound, higher than the nourishing air; we
    have enormous privilege, we do not fear you,

We have invented the jet-plane and the death-bomb and
    the cross of Christ—"Oh," he said, "surely
You'll live forever"—grinning like a skull, covering his
    mouth with his hand—"What could exterminate
    you?"

Ode to Hengist and Horsa

Recently in the south of England
A Saxon warrior was found in the rich earth there, old
    hero bones
Of a man seven feet tall, buried with honor
Under his shield, his spear beside him, and at his hand
The Saxon knife: but every bone of his body was broken
Lest he come forth and walk. It was their custom.
They did not fear the living but they feared the dead,
The stopped-off battle-fury, the stinking flesh.
They honored and perhaps had loved him, but they broke
    his bones
Lest he come back.
      For life, the natural animal thinks,
    life is the treasure.
No wonder the dead envy it, gnashing their jaws
In the black earth. He was our loyal captain and friend,
But now he is changed, he belongs to another nation,
The grim tribes underground. We break their bones
To hold them down. We must not be destroyed
By the dead or the living. We have all history ahead of
    us.

Star-Swirls

The polar ice-caps are melting, the mountain glaciers
Drip into rivers; all feed the ocean;
Tides ebb and flow, but every year a little bit higher.
They will drown New York, they will drown London.
And this place, where I have planted trees and built a
    stone house,
Will be under sea. The poor trees will perish,
And little fish will flicker in and out the windows. I built
    it well,
Thick walls and Portland cement and gray granite,
The tower at least will hold against the sea's buffeting;
    it will become
Geological, fossil and permanent.
What a pleasure it is to mix one's mind with geological
Time, or with astronomical relax it.
There is nothing like astronomy to pull the stuff out of
    man.
His stupid dreams and red-rooster importance: let him
    count the star-swirls.

Unnatural Powers

For fifty thousand years man has been dreaming of
    powers
Unnatural to him: to fly like the eagles—this groundling!
    —to breathe under the seas, to voyage to the moon,
To launch like the sky-god intolerable thunder-bolts:
    now he has got them.
How little he looks, how desperately scared and excited,
    like a poisonous insect, and no God pities him.

End of the World

When I was young in school in Switzerland, about the
    time of the Boer War,
We used to take it for known that the human race
Would last the earth out, not dying till the planet died.
    I wrote a schoolboy poem
About the last man walking in stoic dignity along the
    dead shore
Of the last sea, alone, alone, alone, remembering all
His racial past. But now I don't think so. They'll die
    faceless in flocks,
And the earth flourish long after mankind is out.

Do You Still Make War?

Do You Still Make War?

I saw a regiment of soldiers shuffling and stumbling,
Holding each other's hands for guidance,
Falling into the ditches, falling on the plain road,
Under orders to garrison the empty city.
The furious light of what killed the city had killed their
    eyes
At three hundred miles' distance. Oh faithful ones
Do you still make war?

The Epic Stars

The heroic stars spending themselves,
Coining their very flesh into bullets for the lost battle,
They must burn out at length like used candles;
And Mother Night will weep in her triumph, taking
    home her heroes.
There is the stuff for an epic poem,
This magnificent raid at the heart of darkness, this lost
    battle—
We don't know enough, we'll never know.
Oh happy Homer, taking the stars and the gods for
    granted.

Monument

Erase the lines: I pray you not to love classifications:
The thing is like a river, from source to sea-mouth
One flowing life. We that have the honor and hardship
    of being human
Are one flesh with the beasts, and the beasts with the
    plants
One streaming sap, and certainly the plants and algae
    and the earth they spring from
Are one flesh with the stars. The classifications
Are mostly a kind of *memoria technica,* use it but don't
    be fooled.
It is all truly one life, red blood and tree-sap,
Animal, mineral, sidereal, one stream, one organism, one
    God.
There is nothing to be despised nor hated nor feared.
When the third world-war comes, do it well. Kill. Kill
    your brothers. Why not?
God's on both sides. Make a monument of it:
There were never so many people so suddenly killed. We
    can spare millions, millions,
The chiefs in the Kremlin think, and I too. Man's life's
Too common to be lamented; and if they died after a while
    in their beds
It would be nearly as painful—death's never pleasant.
May the terror be brief—but for a people to be defeated
    is worse.

Prophets

The dynamite craters at Fort Ord where they train sol-
diers; and the howling jet-planes
Tearing the sky over this quiet countryside, shaking the
mountain
When one of them over-passes the speed of sound;
The roaring factories these monsters come from; the
snoring voice of huge Asia
Waking from sleep; the hidden and deadly struggles for
power in unholy Russia;
The metal seeds of unearthly violence stored in neat
rows on shelves, waiting the day:
Our prophets forecast an unquiet future.
Do it again. Dumfound the prophets again, prove our
knowledge false. We know that as civilization
Advances, so wars increase. We know that this century
Is devoted to world-wars; we know that an armaments-
race makes war. To heap up weapons—what weap-
ons!—
On both sides of a fence makes war certain as sunrise—
Do it again my dear, April-fool us again, prove the
prophets false!
              Alas that you cannot do it.
You can dance on men's minds, but the deep instincts,
Fear, envy, loyalty, pride of kind and the killer's passion,
are past your power. They are terribly in earnest,
And the other mere speculation. No wonder they are
earnest: for ages
Beyond reckoning those who retain them have killed or

enslaved those who renounce them. It's a bitter saying that war
Will be won by the worst, what else can I say? —Laugh
at *that,* Puck.

To Kill in War Is Not Murder

To kill in war is not murder, but this is not war.
Shooting missiles to the moon—childish romance put
　　into action—calculating the bomb-size
That will completely obliterate New York and Moscow
　　and the polar ice-cap: they have a new breed of men
Working at this. Obedient, intelligent, trained techni-
　　cians like trained seals, tell them to do something
And they can do it. But never ask them their reasons,
For they know nothing. They would break up into neo-
　　Christian jargon like Einstein.

　　　As for me, I am growing old and have never
Been quite so vulgar. I look around at the present world
　　and think of my little grandchildren
To live in it. What? Should I cut their throats?
The beauty of men is dead, or defaced and sarcophagussed
Under vile caricatures: the enormous inhuman
Beauty of things goes on, the beauty of God, the eternal
　　beauty, and perhaps they'll see it.

How Beautiful It Is

It flows out of mystery into mystery: there is no begin-
    ning—
How could there be? And no end—how could there be?
The stars shine in the sky like the spray of a wave
Rushing to meet no shore, and the great music
Blares on forever, but to us very soon
It will be blind. Not we nor our children nor the human
    race
Are destined to live forever, the breath will fail,
The eyes will break—perhaps of our own explosive bile
Vented upon each other—or a stingy peace
Makes parents fools—but far greater witnesses
Will take our places. It is only a little planet
But how beautiful it is.

Birth and Death

I am old and in the ordinary course of nature shall die
    soon, but the human race is not old
But rather childish, it is an infant and acts like one.
And now it has captured the keys of the kingdoms of un-
    earthly violence. Will it use them? It loves destruc-
    tion you know.
And the earth is too small to feed us, we must have room.
It seems expedient that not as of old one man, but many
    nations and races die for the people.
Have you noticed meanwhile the population explosion
Of man on earth, the torrents of new-born babies, the
    bursting schools? Astonishing. It saps man's dignity.
We used to be individuals, not populations.
Perhaps we are now preparing for the great slaughter.
    No reason to be alarmed; stone-dead is dead;
Breeding like rabbits we hasten to meet the day.

The Beautiful Captive

It is curious I cannot feel it yet.

To pile up weapons on both sides of a ditch makes war
     certain as sunrise

Yet I can't feel its approach.

There have been two, there will be a third, to be fought
     with what weapons? These that we test and stock-
     pile.

And every test makes the earth

At such and such a place uninhabitable. We must not
     test them too much, they are too deadly,

We store them. If ours and theirs

Went off at once they'd probably infect the elements and
     blight the whole earth. We have general death on
     our hands,

But wait ten years of peace we'll have more.

Do you think we'll not use them? When a great nation
     in trouble—when a great nation is in danger of be-
     ing conquered

It will use the whole arsenal.

So—be prepared to die. Those whom the blasts miss, the
     air and water will poison them. Those who survive,

Their children will be dying monsters.

I have thought for a long time that we are too many—
     three thousand million is it?—this will adjust us.

I have pitied the beautiful earth

Ridden by such a master as the human race. Now, if we
     die like the dinosaurs, the beautiful

Planet will be the happier.

She is not domesticated, she weeps in her service, the

lovely forehead bowed down to the sleek knees—
Or is she laughing? Good luck to her.
But this fantastic third world-war and self-destruction:
    curious I cannot feel them yet. The idea is logical
But not intuitive: distrust it.
However—if not thus—God will find other means. The
    troublesome race of man, Oh beautiful planet, is
    not immortal.

Memoranda

Let Them Alone

If God has been good enough to give you a poet
Then listen to him. But for God's sake let him alone un-
    til he is dead; no prizes, no ceremony,
They kill the man. A poet is one who listens
To nature and his own heart; and if the noise of the
    world grows up around him, and if he is tough
    enough,
He can shake off his enemies but not his friends.
That is what withered Wordsworth and muffled Tenny-
    son, and would have killed Keats; that is what makes
Hemingway play the fool and Faulkner forget his art.

To the Story-Tellers

Man, the illogical animal. The others go wrong by anach-
  ronistic
Instinct, for the world changes, or mistaken
Observation, but man, his loose moods disjoin; madness
  is under the skin
To the deep bone. He will be covetous
Beyond use or cause, and then suddenly spendthrift flings
  all possessions
To all the spoilers. He will suffer in patience
Until his enemy has him by the throat helpless, and go
  mad with rage
When it least serves. Or he'll murder his love
And feast his foe. Oh—an amazing animal, by education
And instinct: he often destroys himself
For no reason at all, and desperately crawls for life when
  it stinks.
And only man will deny known truth.
You story-tellers, novelist, poet and playwright, have a
  free field,
There are no fences, man will do anything.

Eager to Be Praised

Goethe, they say, was a great poet, Pindar, perhaps, was
a great poet, Shakespeare and Sophocles
Stand beyond question. I am thinking of the few, the
fortunate,
Who died fulfilled.
I think of Christopher Marlowe,
stabbed through the eye in a tavern brawl by a
bawdy serving-man,
Spilling his youth and brains on the greasy planks. I
think of young Keats,
Wild with his work unfinished, sobbing for air, dying in
Rome. I think of Edgar Poe
And Robert Burns. I think of Lucretius leaving his poem
unfinished to go and kill himself. I think of Archi-
lochus
Grinning with crazy bitterness. I think of Virgil
In despair of his life-work, begging his friends to destroy
it, coughing his lungs out.

Yet the young men
Still come to me with their books and manuscripts,
Eager to be poets, eager to be praised, eager as Keats.
They are mad I think.

On an Anthology of Chinese Poems

Beautiful the hanging cliff and the wind-thrown cedars,
    but they have no weight.
Beautiful the fantastically
Small farmhouse and ribbon of rice-fields a mile below;
    and billows of mist
Blow through the gorge. These men were better
Artists than any of ours, and far better observers. They
    loved landscape
And put man in his place. But why
Do their rocks have no weight? They loved rice-wine and
    peace and friendship,
Above all they loved landscape and solitude,
—Like Wordsworth. But Wordsworth's mountains have
    weight and mass, dull though the song be.
It is a moral difference perhaps?

Tear Life to Pieces

Eagle and hawk with their great claws and hooked heads
Tear life to pieces; vulture and raven wait for death to
    soften it.
The poet cannot feed on this time of the world
Until he has torn it to pieces, and himself also.

Believe History

I think we are the ape's children, but believe history
We are the Devil's: the fire-deaths, the flaying alive,
The blinding with hot iron, the crucifixions, the castra-
    tions, the famous
Murder of a King of England by hot iron forced
Through the anus to burn the bowels, and men outside
    the ten-foot dungeon-wall
Could hear him howling. Through such violence, such
    horrors
We have come and survived time.
"It came from the Devil and will go to the Devil,"
The old Norman said.
                   But those were the violences
Of youth. We are not returned to that point.
These are the grim and weeping horrors of old age.

Full Moon

Our eyes by day are good enough: only the birds
Have better sight: but in the dark nights
Foxes may flit around us and we never see them, or a
    lion.
We'd stumble into his jaws. Therefore
Man sleeps at night, huddled behind the stones and the
    fire-coals,
Helpless afraid. Then comes the full moon,
That great red-golden disk rises in the evening to glow
All night long, it is night but we see;
The girls and boys escape from their fathers' tyranny to
    meet in the woods.
The flying witches whistle in the wind
And wild dogs howl. You would be amazed what the
    moon does to us.
Our women come in heat once a month
Following the moon, remembering their outlaw joys in
    the forest;
Our maniacs lift up their heads and howl
And beat their cell-doors, they cannot sleep at full moon,
    they are moon-struck.
Nor can the astronomer see his moon-dazzled
Constellations: let him give one night in the month to
    earth and the moon,
Women and games. Also the ocean-tides
Rise wild and higher, the fierce black water like a tame
    tiger follows her feet
Bearing her beautiful brand on his face.

The Dog in the Sky

Signs have appeared in heaven, that dog is one. The
   second
General war was the end of a period,
The last monstrous convulsion. Now a new age begins.
We'll be wishing ourselves back in the stone age
Or in that comfortable time when Rome fell and the
   dark ages
Danced on its grave. There'll be no more dancing,
But if you are strong enough you can live and die. It is a
   little hard
That the world should change in my old age—never
   mind—we'll meet it.

The Monstrous Drought

Little green tree-frogs—they are less than half the size of
    my thumb—
Pervade the place with their croaking prophecies.
What they say is, "Rain, rain: Here it is, just at hand,
Come and make love." Little fools: this
Is the monstrous drought: it has not rained since last
    winter and now's
Christmas again.

Oysters

On the wide Texan and New Mexican ranches
They call them prairie oysters, but here on the Pacific
    coast-range,
Mountain oysters. The spring round-up was finished,
The calves had been cut and branded and their ears
    notched,
And staggered with their pain up the mountain. A vast
    rose and gold sunset, very beautiful, made in April,
Moved overhead. The men had gone down to the ranch-
    house,
But three old men remained by the dying branding-fire
At the corral gate, Lew Clark and Gilchrist
And Onofrio the Indian; they searched the trampled
Earth by the fire, gathering the testicles of gelded bull-
    calves
Out of the bloody dust; they peeled and toasted them
Over the dying branding-fire and chewed them down,
Grinning at each other, believing that the masculine
    glands
Would renew youth.
                The unhappy calves bawled in
    their pain and their mothers answered them.
The vast sunset, all colored, all earnest, all golden with-
    drew a little higher but made a fierce heart
Against the sea-line, spouting a sudden red glare like the
    eye of God. The old men
Chewed at their meat. I do not believe the testicles of
    bull-calves
Will make an old man young again, but if they could—

What fools those old men are. Age brings hard burdens,
But at worst cools hot blood and sets men free
From the sexual compulsions that madden youth.
Why would they dip their aging bodies again
Into that fire? For old men death's the fire,
Let them dream beautiful death, not women's loins.

Savagely Individual

Heavy and yellow with the clay wrack from the flooded
    valley
The river forces itself into the sea
Not mixing in it, a long crude-ochre serpent outlined
    with foam
Splitting the blue-black ocean. Thus a man through the
    mass of men
Forces his way, savagely individual,
It is only saints and idiots forget themselves. However
The ocean waters will take him
        soon, dead or alive.

The Silent Shepherds

What's the best life for a man?
—Never to have been born, sings the choros, and the
next best
Is to die young. I saw the Sybil at Cumae
Hung in her cage over the public street—
What do you want, Sybil? I want to die.
Apothanein Thelo. Apothanein Thelo. Apothanein
Thelo . . .
You have got your wish. But I meant life, not death.
What's the best life for a man? To ride in the wind. To
ride horses and herd cattle
In solitary places above the ocean on the beautiful moun-
tain, and come home hungry in the evening
And eat and sleep. He will live in the wild wind and
quick rain, he will not ruin his eyes with reading,
Nor think too much.
However, we must have philosophers.
I will have shepherds for my philosophers,
Tall dreary men lying on the hills all night
Watching the stars, let their dogs watch the sheep. And
I'll have lunatics
For my poets, strolling from farm to farm, wild liars dis-
torting
The county news into supernaturalism—
For all men to such minds are devils or gods—and that
increases
Man's dignity, man's importance, necessary lies
Best told by fools.
I will have no lawyers nor constables

Each man guard his own goods: there will be man-
    slaughter,
But no more wars, no more mass-sacrifice. Nor I'll have
    no doctors,
Except old women gathering herbs on the mountain,
Let each have her sack of opium to ease the death-pains.

That would be a good world, free and out-doors.
But the vast hungry spirit of the time
Cries to his chosen that there is nothing good
Except discovery, experiment and experience and dis-
    covery: To look truth in the eyes,
To strip truth naked, let our dogs do our living for us
But man discover.
                    It is a fine ambition,
But the wrong tools. Science and mathematics
Run parallel to reality, they symbolize it, they squint at it,
They never touch it: consider what an explosion
Would rock the bones of men into little white fragments
    and unsky the world
If any mind should for a moment touch truth.

Storm Dance of the Sea Gulls

The storm blowing up, rain and dark weather and the
    roaring wind,
And the gulls making their storm-dance—
They fly low mostly, but now they have gone up into the
    sky,
Whirling and dancing, the common sea gulls,
Believe me, there is nothing there for your hungry beaks,
    no little fish,
No floating corpses, it is all a waste desert of air,
High in the air—
Gray wings and white, floating over the storm,
What are you doing? There is no food up there. —For
    pure beauty of the storm—
They feel the beauty of things—as we do—they give
    their flying hearts to it—their wing-borne hun-
    gers——

My Loved Subject

Old age clawed me with his scaly clutch
As if I had never been such.
I cannot walk the mountains as I used to do
But my subject is what it used to be: my love, my loved
      subject:
Mountain and ocean, rock, water and beasts and trees
Are the protagonists, the human people are only sym-
      bolic interpreters—
So let them live or die. They may in fact
Die rather quickly, if the great manners of death
      dreamed up
In the laboratories work well.

He Is All

There is no God but God; he is all that exists,
And being alone does strangely.
                              He is like an old Basque
      shepherd,
Who was brought to California fifty years ago
And has always been alone, he talks to himself,
Solitude has got into his brain,
Beautiful and terrible things come from his mind.
                              God is a man of war,
Whom can he strike but himself? God is a great poet:
Whom can he praise but himself?

Look, How Beautiful

There is this infinite energy, the power of God forever
    working—toward what purpose? —toward none.
This is God's will; he works, he grows and changes, he
    has no object.
No more than a great sculptor who has found a ledge
    fine of marble, and lives beside it, and carves great
    images,
And casts them down. That is God's will: to make great
    things and destroy them, and make great things
And destroy them again. With war and plague and hor-
    ror, and the diseases of trees and the corruptions of
    stone
He destroys all that stands. But look how beautiful—
Look how beautiful are all the things that He does. His
    signature
Is the beauty of things.

Autobiographical

Patronymic

What ancestor of mine in wet Wales or wild Scotland
Was named Godfrey?—from which by the Anglo-French
    erosion
Geoffrey, Jeffry's son, Jeffries, Jeffers in Ireland—
A totally undistinguished man; the whirlwinds of history
Passed him and passed him by. They marked him no
    doubt,
Hurt him or helped him, they rolled over his head
And he I suppose fought back, but entirely unnoticed;
Nothing of him remains.
                I should like to meet him,
And sit beside him, drinking his muddy beer,
Talking about the Norman nobles and parish politics
And the damned foreigners: I think his tales of woe
Would be as queer as ours, and even farther
From reality. His mind was as quick as ours
But perhaps even more credulous.
                     He was a Christian
No doubt—I am not dreaming back into prehistory—
And christened Godfrey, which means the peace of God.
He never in his life found it, when he died it found him.
He has been dead six or eight centuries,
Mouldering in some forgotten British graveyard, nettles
    and rain-slime.

Nettlebed: I remember a place in Oxfordshire,
That prickly name, I have twisted and turned on a bed
    of nettles

All my life long: an apt name for life: nettlebed.
Deep under it swim the dead, down the dark tides and
bloodshot eras of time, bathed in God's peace.

Fierce Music

All night long the rush and trampling of water
And hoarse withdrawals, the endless ocean throwing his
   skirmish-lines against granite,
Come to my ears and stop there. I have heard them so
   long
That I don't hear them—or have to listen before I hear
   them— How long? Forty years.
But that fierce music has gone on for a thousand
Millions of years. Oh well, we get our share. But weep
   that we lose so much
Because mere use won't cover up the glory.
We have our moments: but mostly we are too tired to
   hear and too dull to see.

Harder than Granite

It is a pity the shock-waves
Of the present population-explosion must push in here
  too.
They will certainly within a century
Eat up the old woods I planted and throw down my
  stonework: Only the little tower,
Four-foot-thick-walled and useless may stand for a time.
That and some verses. It is curious that flower-soft verse
Is sometimes harder than granite, tougher than a steel
  cable, more alive than life.

Cremation

It nearly cancels my fear of death, my dearest said,
When I think of cremation. To rot in the earth
Is a loathsome end, but to roar up in flame—besides, I
    am used to it,
I have flamed with love or fury so often in my life,
No wonder my body is tired, no wonder it is dying.
We had great joy of my body. Scatter the ashes.

Granddaughter

And here's a portrait of my granddaughter Una
When she was two years old: a remarkable painter,
A perfect likeness; nothing tricky nor modernist,
Nothing of the artist fudging his art into the picture,
But simple and true. She stands in a glade of trees with
    a still inlet
Of blue ocean behind her. Thus exactly she looked then,
A forgotten flower in her hand, those great blue eyes
Asking and wondering.
                Now she is five years old

And found herself; she does not ask any more but com-
    mands,
Sweet and fierce-tempered; that light red hair of hers
Is the fuse for explosions. When she is eighteen
I'll not be here. I hope she will find her natural elements,
Laughter and violence; and in her quiet times
The beauty of things—the beauty of transhuman things,
Without which we are all lost. I hope she will find
Powerful protection and a man like a hawk to cover her.

Nightpiece

If you keep command of yourself
You can hear almost anything. But man must rest,
A man must sleep: that is, abandon control: then all the
    sick demons
Take him in charge. Who ever heard of a pleasant dream?
Fear and remorse are monstrously exaggerated,
And fear of responsibility: that is what drags us
Out of our beds into the bitter black night
To walk the floor and shudder and regain control,
Else we should lie and scream. I seem to hear in the
    nights
Many estimable people screaming like babies.
I bite my lips and feel my way to the window,
Where the moon rakes through cloud, the wind pants
    like a dog and the ocean
Tears at his shore, gray claws of a great cat
Slitting the granite. The elements thank God are well
    enough,
It is only man must be always wakeful, steering through
    hell.

Vulture

I had walked since dawn and lay down to rest on a bare
  hillside
Above the ocean. I saw through half-shut eyelids a vul-
  ture wheeling high up in heaven,
And presently it passed again, but lower and nearer, its
  orbit narrowing, I understood then
That I was under inspection. I lay death-still and heard
  the flight-feathers
Whistle above me and make their circle and come nearer.
I could see the naked red head between the great wings
Bear downward staring. I said, "My dear bird, we are
  wasting time here.
These old bones will still work; they are not for you."
  But how beautiful he looked, gliding down
On those great sails; how beautiful he looked, veering
  away in the sea-light over the precipice. I tell you
  solemnly
That I was sorry to have disappointed him. To be eaten
  by that beak and become part of him, to share those
  wings and those eyes—
What a sublime end of one's body, what an enskyment;
  what a life after death.

Salvage

It is true that half the glory is gone.
Motors and modernist houses usurp the scene.
There is no eagle soaring, nor a puma
On the Carmel hill highroad, where thirty years ago
We watched one pass. Yet by God's grace
I have still a furlong of granite cliff, on which the Pa-
cific
Leans his wild weight; and the trees I planted
When I was young, little green whips in hand,
Have grown on despite of the biting sea-wind,
And are accepted by nature, an angry-voiced tribe of
night-herons'
Nests on the boughs. One has to pay for it;
The county taxes take all my income, and it seems ridic-
ulous
To hold three acres of shorelong woodland
And the little low house that my own hands made, at the
annual cost
Of a shiny new car. Never mind, the trees and the stones
are worth it.
But it's darker now. I am old, and my wife has died,
Whose eyes made life. As for me, I have to consider and
take thought
Before I can feel the beautiful secret
In places and stars and stones. To her it came freely.
I wish that all human creatures might feel it.
That would make joy in the world, and make men per-
haps a little nobler—as a handful of wildflowers,
Is nobler than the human race.

But I Am Growing Old and Indolent

I have been warned. It is more than thirty years since I
    wrote—
Thinking of the narrative poems I made, which always
Ended in blood and pain, though beautiful enough—my
    pain, my blood,
They were my creatures—I understood, and wrote to
    myself:
"Make sacrifices once a year to magic
Horror away from the house"—for that hangs imminent
Over all men and all houses— "This little house here
You have built over the ocean with your own hands
Beside the standing sea-boulders . . ." So I listened
To my Demon warning me that evil would come
If my work ceased, if I did not make sacrifice
Of storied and imagined lives, Tamar and Cawdor
And Thurso's wife—"imagined victims be our re-
    deemers"—
At that time I was sure of my fates and felt
My poems guarding the house, well-made watchdogs
Ready to bite.
            But time sucks out the juice,
A man grows old and indolent.

Hand

Fallen in between the tendons and bones
It looks like a dead hand. Poor hand a little longer
Write, and see what comes forth from a dead hand.

See the Human Figure

As the eye fails through age or disease
And the world grows a little dark it begins to have hu-
man figures in it.
A stone on the mountain has a man's face,
A storm-warped tree against the fog on the mountain is a
man running, hopelessly,
Fleeing his fear; and at night by candle light
A huddle of bed-clothes on the bed is visibly a woman
dying, that dearest
Woman who has been dead for ten years.
The eye's tricks are strange, the mind has to be quick
and resolute or you'll believe in them
And be gabbling with ghosts. For take note that
They are always human: to see the human figure in all
things is man's disease;
To see the inhuman God is our health.

My Burial Place

I have told you in another poem, whether you've read it
    or not,
About a beautiful place the hard-wounded
Deer go to die in; their bones lie mixed in their little
    graveyard
Under leaves by a flashing cliff-brook, and if
They have ghosts they like it, the bones and mixed ant-
    lers are well content.
Now comes for me the time to engage
My burial place: put me in a beautiful place far off from
    men,
No cemetery, no necropolis,
And for God's sake no columbarium, nor yet no funeral.

But if the human animal were precious
As the quick deer or that hunter in the night the lonely
    puma
I should be pleased to lie in one grave with 'em.

Ghost

There is a jaggle of masonry here, on a small hill
Above the gray-mouthed Pacific, cottages and a thick-
    walled tower, all made of rough sea-rock
And Portland cement. I imagine, fifty years from now,
A mist-gray figure moping about this place in mad moon-
    light, examining the mortar-joints, pawing the
Parasite ivy: "Does the place stand? How did it take that
    last earthquake?" Then someone comes
From the house-door, taking a poodle for his bedtime
    walk. The dog snarls and retreats; the man
Stands rigid, saying "Who are you? What are you doing
    here?" "Nothing to hurt you," it answers, "I am just
    looking
At the walls that I built. I see that you have played hell
With the trees that I planted." "There has to be room
    for people," he answers. "My God," he says, "*That*
    still!"

APPENDIX

Three Uncollected Poems

———

Animula

The immortality of the soul—
God save us from it! To live for seventy years is a bur-
    den—
To live eternally, poor little soul—
Not the chief devil could inflict nor endure it. Fortu-
    nately
We are not committed, there is no danger.
Our consciousness passes into the world's perhaps, but
    that
Being infinite can endure eternity.
—Words, theological words—eternal, infinite—we dream
    too much.
But the beauty of God is high, clear and visible,
Hauteclaire like Roland's sword, the cliffs, the ocean, the
    sunset cloud
Blood-red and smoky amber, strong ochre
And faint spring green: but presently come the stars, and
    we are too small.
Man's world puffs up his mind, as a toad
Puffs himself up; the billion light-years cause a serene
    and wholesome deflation.

The Shears

A great dawn-color rose widening the petals around her
    gold eye
Peers day and night in the window. She watches us
Breakfasting, lighting lamps, reading, and the children
    playing, and the dogs by the fire,
She watches earnestly, uncomprehending,
As we stare into the world of trees and roses uncompre-
    hending,
There is a great gulf fixed. But even while
I gaze, and the rose at me, my little flower-greedy
    daughter-in-law
Walks with shears, very blonde and housewifely
Through the small garden, and suddenly the rose finds
    herself rootless in-doors.
Now she is part of the life she watched.
—So we: death comes and plucks us: we become part of
    the living earth
And wind and water whom we so loved. We are they.

Birds and Fishes

Every October millions of little fish come along the shore,
Coasting this granite edge of the continent
On their lawful occasions: but what a festival for the sea-
   fowl.
What a witches' sabbath of wings
Hides the dark water. The heavy pelicans shout "Haw!"
   like Job's friend's warhorse
And dive from the high air, the cormorants
Slip their long black bodies under the water and hunt
   like wolves
Through the green half-light. Screaming, the gulls
   watch,
Wild with envy and malice, cursing and snatching. What
   hysterical greed!
What a filling of pouches! the mob
Hysteria is nearly human—these decent birds!—as if
   they were finding
Gold in the street. It is better than gold,
It can be eaten: and which one in all this fury of wild-
   fowl pities the fish?
No one certainly. Justice and mercy
Are human dreams, they do not concern the birds nor the
   fish nor eternal God.
However—look again before you go.
The wings and the wild hungers, the wave-worn skerries,
   the bright quick minnows
Living in terror to die in torment—
Man's fate and theirs—and the island rocks and immense
   ocean beyond, and Lobos

Darkening above the bay: they are beautiful?
That is their quality: not mercy, not mind, not goodness,
   but the beauty of God.

About the Author

ROBINSON JEFFERS died in 1962 at the age of seventy-five, ending one of the most controversial poetic careers of this century. The present book is his twenty-first book of verse, dating from *Flagons and Apples* (1912), and his first since *Hungerfield* (1954).

The son of a theology professor at Western Seminary in Pittsburgh, Jeffers was taught Greek, Latin, and Hebrew as a boy, and spent three years in Germany and Switzerland before entering the University of Western Pennsylvania (now Pittsburgh) at fifteen. His education continued on the West Coast after his parents moved there, and he graduated from Occidental College at eighteen. His interest in forestry, medicine, and general science led him to pursue his studies at the University of Southern California, and at the University of Zurich.

Jeffers received a small legacy from a distant cousin in Pittsburgh, married (1913), and bought land in Carmel, California. He built Tor House there with rocks which he dragged from the beach, taking four years to complete the basic structure. All the while he was writing poetry, and his first major work, *Tamar and Other Poems,* was published in 1924, with *Roan Stallion* following in 1925.

Among Jeffers' other major works are *The Woman at Point Sur* (1927); *Cawdor* (1928); *Descent to the Dead* (1931); *Thurso's Landing* (1932); *Give Your Heart to the Hawks* (1933); *Solstice* (1935); *Such Counsels You Gave to Me* (1937); *Medea* (1946)—the successful Broadway play; and *The Double Axe* (1948).